W9-AUS-736

HUMMINGBIRDS

Jolyon Goddard

Grolier
an imprint of
SCHOLASTIC
www.scholastic.com/librarypublishing

Published 2008 by Grolier
An imprint of Scholastic Library Publishing
Old Sherman Turnpike, Danbury,
Connecticut 06816

For The Brown Reference Group plc
Project Editor: Jolyon Goddard
Copy-editors: Lesley Ellis, Lisa Hughes, Wendy Horobin
Picture Researcher: Clare Newman
Designers: Jeni Child, Lynne Ross, Sarah Williams
Managing Editor: Bridget Giles

Volume ISBN-13: 978-0-7172-6257-1
Volume ISBN-10: 0-7172-6257-X

Library of Congress Cataloging-in-Publication Data

Nature's children. Set 2.
p. cm.
Includes bibliographical references and index.
ISBN-13: 978-0-7172-8081-0
ISBN-10: 0-7172-8081-0
1. Animals--Encyclopedias, Juvenile. I. Grolier (Firm)
QL49.N383 2007
590--dc22
2007026928

Printed and bound in China

PICTURE CREDITS

Front Cover: **Shutterstock**: Ronnie Howard

Back Cover: **Nature PL**: Pete Oxford, Kim Taylor; **Shutterstock**: Natalie Sinjushina and Evgeniy Meyla, Tim Zurowski.

Alamy: Arco Images 9, William Leaman 42; **Corbis**: George D. Lepp 45; **FLPA**: Malcolm Schuyc 22, Konrad Wothe 34; **NHPA**: Stephen Dalton 26–27, Nick Garbutt 10; **Photolibrary.com**: Michael Fogden 29, 30; **Shutterstock**: Gualberto Becerra 46, Bronwyn Photo 14, Ferenc Cegledi 6, Ronnie Howard 5, John L. Richburg 37, Kiyoshi Takahase Segundo 17, Adam Tinney 21, Tim Zurowski 2–3, 4, 13, 18, 22; **Still Pictures**: BIOS/Jany Sauvanet 41, Ed Reschke 38.

Contents

FACT FILE: Hummingbirds

Class	Birds (Aves)
Order	Hummingbirds, swifts, and tree swifts (Apodiformes)
Family	Hummingbirds (Trochilidae)
Genera	There are 109 genera of hummingbirds; 9 genera breed in or visit North America
Species	About 335 species of hummingbirds; 16 species breed in or visit North America, including the ruby-throated hummingbird (*Archilochus colubris*) and rufous hummingbird (*Selasphorus rufus*)
World distribution	Hummingbirds occur naturally only in North and South America
Habitat	Gardens, pastures, woods, and tropical forests
Distinctive physical characteristics	Small flying birds with long wings and brightly colored feathers; long, thin beak; small legs
Habits	Hover when feeding; become torpid at night; female raises young in a nest
Diet	Mainly nectar; insects; some hummingbirds drink tree sap

Introduction

Hummingbirds are one of nature's most amazing birds. All hummingbirds are small and many are brightly colored. For example, the ruby-throated hummingbird, which lives in North America, has a patch of brilliant red feathers on its throat. Hummingbirds move incredibly quickly and are very acrobatic. To dip their long thin beak into the heart of a flower, they hover in midair. Their wings beat so fast that they appear to be a blur surrounding the floating bird. They can even fly backward! There are many different types of hummingbirds, and they live in a wide range of places, from tropical forests in South and Central America to backyards in North America.

A ruby-throated hummingbird's wings beat 55 times each second as it hovers.

The Amazilia hummingbird lives in Peru.

Big Family

After flycatchers, hummingbirds make up the biggest family of birds, with about 335 **species**, or types. Wherever red flowers bloom in North and South America, there are sure to be hummingbirds, too. These birds do not live naturally in Europe, Asia, Africa, or Australia. Although the sunbirds of Africa can hover like hummingbirds, they are not closely related.

Most types of hummingbirds live in the tropics. But some venture as far north as Alaska or as far south as Tierra del Fuego at the bottom tip of South America. Hummingbirds live in various types of places, or habitats, including mountains, pastures, forests, and backyards.

Sixteen species of hummingbirds visit or breed in North America. The most well-known of the North American species are the ruby-throated hummingbird and the rufous hummingbird. The ruby-throated hummingbird breeds in eastern North America. The rufous hummingbird breeds in western North America.

Great and Small

The smallest hummingbird is also the tiniest bird in the world. The bee hummingbird lives in Cuba. It weighs less than one-tenth of an ounce (2 g). From the tip of its beak to the end of its tail is about 2½ inches (6 cm) long. The biggest member of the family is the giant hummingbird. It lives in the Andes of South America. It weighs about four-fifths of an ounce (22 g). Though still light, that's ten times as heavy as the bee hummingbird.

Like many other birds, male hummingbirds are more colorful and fancier than the females. The males often have dazzling patches of feathers. Some males have spiky crests on their head or a showy tail. These decorations help them win over females in the breeding season. The muted feathers of the females allow them to remain unseen in their nest when they raise their **chicks**. That way the females can avoid attention from predators such as snakes and birds of prey.

The giant hummingbird's feathers are dull compared to the feathers of most other hummingbirds.

This is a close-up of the feathers of the white-necked jacobin, a hummingbird from Central and South America.

Fantastic Feathers

Hummingbirds often look like they have colorful fish scales rather than feathers. Birds do have scales, actually, but just on their legs. Hummingbirds have small feathers, many of which are **iridescent**. That means when you look at them from different angles, the feathers shimmer and appear to be many different colors. The word *iridescent* comes from the Greek word for "rainbow."

What makes the hummingbirds' feathers iridescent? The smallest parts of a feather are called barbules. Those are made up of many tiny plates. These plates are filled with air bubbles. Light reflects on these plates much like it does on a soap bubble that has the colors of the rainbow swirling on its surface. As the bird turns in the sunlight, the feathers appear to change color. The feathers might appear to be a rich violet one second, then a dazzling red the next.

Flight of Fancy

Hummingbirds are truly fantastic fliers. They don't have to run or jump to take off like other birds. Hummingbirds can hover, make sharp turns in midair, and even fly sideways and backward. They reach full speed almost immediately and can stop abruptly.

For such a small bird, hummingbirds fly very fast. They can reach speeds of 40 miles per hour (65 km/h). When diving, they can reach even faster speeds—up to 60 miles per hour (90 km/h)!

A hummingbird has powerful flight muscles. They make up almost one-third of the bird's weight. Birds have two sets of flight muscles. One set of muscles lifts the wings and the other set pulls them down. In most birds, the muscles that pull down the wings are much bigger and stronger. But in hummingbirds both sets are powerful. That lets the bird beat its wings up to 80 times a second when hovering. The wings beat so fast that they look like a blur.

A hummingbird can move only by flying. Its legs are too weak for walking.

Hummingbirds are named for the humming sound their beating wings make.

Wonderful Wings

A hummingbird's wings are the equivalent of our arms. Whereas humans have long arm bones and short hand bones, hummingbirds have the opposite. The hand part of the wing is large in hummingbirds. The arm bones are very short and form a V shape. The joint between the V and the bird's shoulder lets the wing rotate in many directions, not just up and down. The wing tips can twist and turn like a boat paddle, propelling through air instead of water. This freedom of movement allows hummingbirds to be very acrobatic in flight. Hummingbirds have even been known to make backward somersaults in midair and fly upside down!

The wings trace different patterns in the air for different maneuvers. For example, when hovering the hummingbird's wing tips trace figure-eights in the air. To fly backward the hummingbird holds its wings behind its body, tilts them upward, and makes a circular movement with them.

Energetic Birds

Flying takes a lot of energy. And because hummingbirds beat their wings so much, they use more energy than any other bird or mammal. In the whole of the animal kingdom, only certain insects use more energy for flying. A hummingbird's heart beats incredibly fast to pump oxygen-rich blood to the bird's flight muscles. The heart rate has been measured at 1,260 beats per minute—that's 21 beats per second—in a blue-throated hummingbird!

Hummingbirds lose heat quickly from their body because they are small. They also do not have an inner layer of soft, downy feathers that keep heat in, like most other birds have.

A hummingbird needs a lot of high-energy food. It must eat at least half its body weight in food each day just to survive.

A hummingbird can hover for up to 50 minutes in one place.

A pair of Anna's hummingbirds sip nectar.

Nice Nectar

Hummingbirds spend most of their day feeding. Their favorite food is **nectar**. Nectar is a sweet sugar-water made by flowers. It is found deep inside the bloom. A hummingbird sucks the nectar out with its long tongue. During feeding, the hummingbird spends almost all its time searching for and sipping nectar. However, the birds also spend some time eating insects. That gives them essential protein. The birds pick off insects from leaves, twigs, and flowers, or catch them in midair.

Wherever there are red flowers in bloom, a hummingbird will have food. In spring the hummingbirds that **migrate** arrive a month before their favorite flowers are out. The hummingbirds would soon die without food. But they have another source of sugar—tree **sap**. The hummingbirds get to the tree sap by poking their long beak into holes in tree trunks. These holes were drilled by other birds called **sapsuckers**.

Flower Friends

North American hummingbirds drink nectar from about 150 different kinds of flowers. Hummingbirds can spot their favorite flowers easily because they are bright orange or red. Bees—other collectors of nectar—cannot see red so they ignore these flowers, which include fuchsias, verbenas, and red hot pokers. However, hummingbirds will also explore different-colored flowers for nectar.

The flowers that hummingbirds like the most are often shaped like bells, trumpets, or tubes. Flying insects find it hard to land on these flowers. However, hummingbirds can hover while sipping the flower's nectar. A hummingbird can easily poke its slender beak into the heart of the flower to get to the nectar.

This hummingbird uses its long, thin beak to reach the flower's nectar.

A hummingbird has large eyes that let the bird see straight ahead and to the sides.

Senses

A hummingbird's most important sense is vision. They have better eyesight than humans. They can also see a wider range of colors, including ultraviolet. However, hummingbirds are especially attracted to the color red. That's because they associate red with nectar-producing flowers. Their hearing is excellent, too. They can hear high-pitched sounds outside the range of what humans can hear.

Hummingbirds use their sense of taste to check how sweet nectar is. That way they will not waste time drinking nectar that does not contain much sugar. The sweeter the nectar, the more energy they will get from it. Their sense of smell is not well developed. Nor is their sense of touch. However, female hummingbirds do use touch during nest-building.

Tongue Twisters

A hummingbird's tongue is longer than the length of its beak. When a hummingbird is not feeding, the base of the tongue is curled up inside the head, near the eyes. During feeding, the tongue uncurls and its end extends out of the tip of the beak. The end of the tongue is divided into two parts. Each part has fringes. Those help lap up nectar. The ruby-throated hummingbird pokes its tongue in and out up to 13 times a second during feeding, to lap up as much nectar as possible.

Do flowers get anything in return for their nectar? Yes! Hummingbirds transfer **pollen** from one flower to the next. Pollen is a sticky, grainy powder. If these grains get onto another flower of the same type, the flower can then produce seeds. Seeds in turn grow into new plants. Because plants cannot move around, they need help. As the hummingbird feeds, pollen brushes onto its feathers. When the bird visits another flower, the pollen brushes off onto the flower.

All Day Long

Hummingbirds use up so much energy that they have to spend all day feeding. Often, they are up before dawn, getting their breakfast from early opening flowers. They keep feeding till after dusk, when other day birds have turned in for the night.

Hummingbirds have a good memory. They remember where their favorite flowers grow and return there each year. Anything red—which they associate with nectar—attracts their attention and they will investigate it. They will even check out a scrap of red cloth or a red drink can. Some hummingbirds are territorial feeders—they find a source of nectar and defend it, chasing away other birds and insects that come near. Other hummingbirds are not so territorial. They happily dart from one flower to the next, sharing them with other birds and insects.

An Amazilia hummingbird checks out a bird-of-paradise flower.

Preening

Every now and then a hummingbird stops feeding to clean itself. It perches on a little branch. The hummingbird uses its beak to ruffle through its feathers, picking out dirt. Finally, the bird **preens** its feathers with oil. The oil is made by a gland near the bird's tail called a **preen gland**. The oil makes the hummingbird's feathers waterproof.

Hummingbirds also need a bath now and then. They have to bathe wherever they find water. Any water will do. They'll press themselves against wet moss or raindrops on a leaf. They'll hover by a waterfall and soak up the spray. They'll dip in pools and streams. After refreshing themselves, hummingbirds fly to a nearby branch and shake off the water.

A green-crowned brilliant hummingbird from Costa Rica bathes in the rain.

A scintillant hummingbird is in torpor for the night.

Torpor

At night, a hummingbird finally stops feeding. It clings onto a perch with its feet. Most birds tuck their head under a wing and sleep that way. Hummingbirds fluff out their feathers, pull in their neck, and point their head up toward the sky.

When you go to sleep at night, your heartbeat and breathing stay much the same as they are during the day. Your body temperature doesn't change much either. To keep things the same, your body uses up energy. Hummingbirds can't afford to waste energy, however. They are unable to store enough energy to keep the same temperature and heart rate through the night.

Luckily the hummingbird has a clever way of saving energy through the night. By fluffing out its feathers, heat escapes and its body cools. Its heart rate and breathing slow. It might breathe just once every few minutes. This state is called **torpor**. The hummingbird saves a lot of energy in this condition.

Summer Vacation

Most types of hummingbirds live in the tropics and stay in the same place all year round. But some types travel north in spring to breed. This seasonal journey is called a migration.

Some hummingbirds that migrate from their winter homes near the equator, stop in the southern United States. Others, however, travel much farther—as far as Canada and Alaska.

The ruby-throated hummingbird travels from Mexico to the eastern United States. Instead of flying overland, it flies 500 miles (800 km) over the Gulf of Mexico—a nonstop flight with no nectar. The journey takes about 25 hours. Before the journey, the birds put on an extra one-tenth of an ounce (2 g) of fat. That's about half of what they already weigh. Migratory hummingbirds return to their winter home in fall when the days begin to shorten.

The rufous hummingbird spends summers as far north as Canada. It migrates to Mexico for winters.

A female broad-billed hummingbird builds a nest.

Nest-building

Before she's even found a mate, a female hummingbird builds a nest. Now that's planning ahead! She needs to time it carefully so that her chicks will hatch when there are plenty of flowers in bloom.

The female builds her nest alone without help from a male hummingbird. It takes her about a week to make it. She makes the nest on a branch, attached to a big leaf, or even in a stone wall. She makes sure the nest is near some flowers that will provide nectar for herself and her chicks when they hatch.

The nest is built from leaves, grass, bark, and plant fibers. Sometimes, the female uses spiderwebs as a kind of glue to hold it all together. To make the inside comfortable, she shapes it into a snug cup. She lines the cup with soft materials such as feathers and soft plant fibers. She finishes the nest by covering the outside with bark or moss. This way the outside is **camouflaged**—it blends into the surroundings so predators will not notice it.

Courtship

Now that her new cozy nest is complete, a female hummingbird looks for a mate. She sits back and watches as male hummingbirds try to impress her.

North American male hummingbirds such as the ruby-throated hummingbird put on a spectacular aerial display to attract females. Males carve out a perfect U shape in the air. They do that repeatedly, dipping low over the female's head. There, she gets a chance to admire his iridescent red throat. The male also makes courtship noises. As the air passes through his wing and tail feathers, it makes a zinging sound. He also moves his feathers briskly to make popping and buzzing noises. Some male hummingbirds make sure they fly facing the Sun so their feathers glitter and sparkle to their full effect.

The dazzling throat of a male hummingbird impresses female hummingbirds during courtship.

The iridescent throat of male hummingbirds, such as this rufous hummingbird, is called a gorget.

Separate Ways

If a female hummingbird is impressed by a male's courtship display, she leads her suitor into the branches of a tree. There, the male flits to and fro in front of her before they mate. Afterward, the male and female go their separate ways. Hummingbirds spend most of their time alone. Other than courting or when a female raises her chicks, hummingbirds have a solitary life.

Many South American male hummingbirds rely more on their voices than their colorful feathers or fanciful flying to attract a mate. That's because in the dense forest in which they live the females cannot easily see dazzling flying displays. Because a single male bird's voice is not very loud, the males come together and sing as a chorus.

Two Eggs

Hummingbirds' eggs are pure white and long. The female lays one egg and then another two days later in her nest. Protecting her nest and eggs is now the female's priority. She chases away any intruder that gets too close.

Sitting on eggs to keep them warm is called incubation. The female spends many hours incubating the eggs. Every now and then she darts off to feed on nectar and insects. But she does not stay away too long. She sleeps at night but does not become torpid. That way she is still aware of any approaching danger.

After two or three weeks of incubation, the baby birds hatch two days apart. The chicks have no feathers and their eyes are tightly shut. They are entirely dependent on their mother for warmth and food.

This nest with eggs belongs to a green-tailed goldenthroat, a hummingbird from South America.

A female ruby-throated hummingbird returns to her two chicks.

Nest Life

Baby hummingbirds have a lot of growing to do and need food. Their mother has a pouch in her beak, which is called a **crop**. In the crop, she stores insects and nectar for her chicks. She darts back and forth to the nest all day. When its mother arrives back at the nest with food the chick opens its beak wide and its mother squirts the contents of her crop into its crop. The chick's crop bulges as though it had a marble stuck in its throat.

Unlike other birds, baby hummingbirds do not grow soft downy feathers. Instead, the chicks remain bald until their adult feathers grow. At night their mother keeps them warm.

The chicks grow fast. The nest soon becomes crowded, but it can stretch as the baby birds grow. After 16 days, a chick's eyes are wide open and its adult feathers have grown in. The chick's flight muscles are now strong. At about this time, the little birds begin to grip the edge of the nest with their feet and practice flapping.

Going Alone

Practice makes perfect, and soon the **nestlings** are **fledglings**. The young hummingbirds let go and hover around the nest. However, they are not ready for life on their own just yet. They need to learn to fend for themselves. They use a branch near the nest as a meeting place. There, the mother feeds her fledglings until they know how to feed themselves.

As soon as her young are independent, the mother hummingbird returns to her solitary way of life. As the days get colder and shorter, North American hummingbirds instinctively know that it is time to migrate south in search of warmth and food. The chicks now lead a lonely adult hummingbird's life, only meeting other hummingbirds for courting and mating.

A young Allen's hummingbird practices flapping its wings.

Hummingbirds, such as this green hermit, are so agile in the air that they can avoid most predators.

Hungry Hunters

Plenty of predators will make a meal of a young hummingbird if given the chance. These hunters include snakes, other birds, and small mammals that can climb trees. The mother hummingbird has to leave the nest to find nectar and insects, but she does not fly far. If an intruder comes, she defends her chicks aggressively.

Once they are out of the nest and flying, the young birds have a good chance of surviving to a ripe old age—hummingbirds can live to at least 10 years. A hungry bird of prey, such as a hawk, might swoop down and catch a hummingbird off guard. But hummingbirds' wings let them dart around with grace and speed. That can help them avoid most predators.

Helping Out

If you live in an area where hummingbirds visit, you can be their friend. By making or buying a hummingbird feeder and hanging it in your backyard, you will be able to see and enjoy hummingbirds close up. You will also be providing the birds with an abundant supply of "man-made nectar"! To attract hummingbirds, the feeder should be red—the same color as their favorite flowers.

To make your own nectar, simply dissolve table sugar in water. Too much sugar would rot your teeth. But that is not a problem for hummingbirds because they don't have teeth! The homemade nectar should remain fresh for up to four days. It is best to feed the hummingbirds just in summer. In cooler weather a cold drink might cool the bird's tiny body too much and send it into torpor.

Words to Know

Camouflaged Colored or shaded to blend in with the background.

Chicks Young birds.

Crop The wide part of a hummingbird's throat. Food is stored in the crop.

Fledglings Young birds that have grown their first adult feathers.

Iridescent Changing color when seen from different angles.

Migrate To move from one place to another regularly in search of food, mates, territory, or warmer weather.

Nectar A sugary liquid made by some flowers.

Nestlings Young birds that cannot yet fly and live in a nest.

Pollen	A sticky powder that flowers make and exchange to produce seeds.
Preen gland	A gland that produces an oily substance that hummingbirds use to waterproof their feathers.
Preens	Cleans and oils feathers.
Sap	A fluid—often sweet—that circulates in plants.
Sapsuckers	Birds that drill holes in trees to drink their sap.
Species	The scientific word for animals of the same type that breed together.
Torpor	A sleeplike state in which a hummingbird's breathing and heart rate slow and its body temperature drops at night.

Find Out More

Books

Aziz, L. *Hummingbirds: A Beginner's Guide.* Toronto, Ontario, Canada. Firefly Books, 2002.

Romeu, E. *The Bee Hummingbird.* Animals of the Americas. Miami, Florida: Santillana USA Publishing Company, 2004.

Web sites

Hummingbird Journey North
www.learner.org/jnorth/tm/humm/jr/JnKidsOverview.html
A ton of information about migrating ruby-throated and rufous hummingbirds.

Ruby-throated Hummingbird
www.iwrc-online.org/kids/Facts/Birds/rubyhum1.htm
Interesting facts about the ruby-throated hummingbird.

Index